FAST TRACK TO RICHE$

By T.J. Rohleder
Founder of the Direct-Response Network

Also by T.J. Rohleder:

Introduction

Hi, this is T. J. Rohleder with M.O.R.E. Inc. in Goessel, Kansas. I'd like to welcome you -- yes, you! -- to the Fast Track to Riches. I'm so glad you've picked up this publication and I think you will be, too -- because inside, I outline an exciting program in which I'll show you the exact steps you need to take in order to **start making tremendous amounts of money in your own business**.

If you've ever been confused about what it really takes to go from almost no money to making millions of dollars, I promise you that you will not be confused by the time you finish reading this publication. I'm going to lay out the entire process for you, more clearly than you've ever had it explained to you before.

You'll find that, in the process, I'll use a lot of examples I've taken from my own life and from the experiences of my close colleagues and friends -- especially a gentleman named Russ von Hoelscher. Russ is a well-known marketing expert, a consultant who charges hundreds of dollars an hour to help other people make money. He came aboard with M.O.R.E., Inc. back in the spring of 1990 and helped us go from bringing in about $16,000 a month in sales -- which we thought was pretty good! -- to **making over $100,000 a week** just nine months later. He's the man who introduced us to a lot of these strategies in the first place.

Russ tells me that the most asked question he gets at seminars, on the phone, by fax, or by mail is, **"How can I get started? What can I do? What can I sell?"** People are excited about going into business for themselves, but they immediately run right up against the brick wall of what to start out with and how to market it. Well, that's what this publication is all about; I'm going to do my best to answer those questions. I'm going to break everything down into four simple steps. I'm not going to promise that it's always going to be easy; that would be a bald-faced lie. **If you really want to be rich, you'll need to work for it** and I'm going to talk about that reality here, too. I'm going to discuss the difference between something that's easy and something that's hard, and how you can make things that are hard now so much easier with a little practice.

That Fateful Question

Everybody wants to know, "How do you become rich?" I swear that if you go down the street and talk to 100 people, asking them whether they would prefer to be financially independent or keep struggling for money, 90% would tell you that they'd rather be financially independent. **Most of the 10% who'd say otherwise are probably lying, unless of course they're afraid of success**. That's a real possibility because a small percentage of people really do have a fear of success; they're afraid things will change between them and their friends and loved ones. **So sure, there are people terrified by the thought of failure; but there are also those who are terrified by the thought of success.**

Most people who would like to be rich just don't know how to get there and, sadly, a lot of the ideas people have about business and generating wealth come from others who've never really done it themselves. **It's that bad advice that can be the real killer.** More than 20 years ago, when I expressed my own desire to get rich, my father told me, **"Son, you can get those ideas right out of your head because, unless you're lucky or you've inherited it,**

you're never going to get rich." If I'd followed that bad advice, and had actually believed that, it would have never happened. **You have to believe it's possible before you can ever do it.** What I'm saying is, you have to reject advice like that from friends and loved ones, no matter how well meaning they are, unless they have some direct experience in attempting to generate wealth or run a business and, even then, you have to take what they say with a grain of salt.

Russ von Hoelscher's story is pretty much the same. When he was starting out over 30 years ago, he'd just gotten married. He was doing a few things part-time in a business of his own, but otherwise he was managing some bookstores and record stores in Minneapolis, St. Paul, and Duluth for somebody else. He tells me his new wife took his mother aside and talked to her, and then the two of them called a meeting with him. They all sat down and the women said, "You seem to be ready to leave your job and go into business for yourself. We want to tell you that we don't think that you should do that. We think you have a great job!" At the time, Russ was making a very big salary plus commissions -- but he decided not to listen to that advice and the rest is history. The moral? **Some of the most well-meaning people can give some of the worst advice.**

That's usually because they don't want to see us get hurt. When my father told me to forget about getting rich, I knew that he simply didn't want to see me suffer like so many do suffer. **I'll be honest: my wife and I struggled for a number of years before we finally found the right plan that took us where we wanted to go**. There we were, barely able to afford to pay our bills; the utility companies kept threatening to turn off our water, gas, and electricity. We were barely able to pay our rent -- and yet we kept sending away for moneymaking programs that promised to show us how to make big bucks. Yes, I know, that can almost seem insane. I realize that a lot of people thought we were crazy, to think that we could get rich when we could barely afford to pay our bills. We kept the faith, though, and that eventually led us to the idea that we were working with when we first met Russ. **We had that burning desire to succeed and we didn't let our families and friends, no matter how well-meaning, or anybody else stand in our way.** And thanks to Russ' help, we've earned millions of dollars since.

That's what you have to do, folks. What could be more depressing than the life of a wage slave -- constantly working for somebody else, never getting ahead, being a robot for someone else's company? People try to protect us and keep us in that rat-race, but when they do, they're actually they're doing us a disservice. **There's no joy, no real life, and no freedom when you're a wage slave.** I think that liberation comes when you strike out on your own, even if you do take a few setbacks. You're still alive. You're striving to achieve something of value. That in itself gives you a sense of truly living, a feeling that's so powerful that it's indescribable. **You have to feel it yourself to understand -- <u>and I'm here to help you get there</u>.**

Chapter One

Taking That First Step

The first step in becoming fabulously wealthy is, quite simply, deciding that you're going to get rich. This preparation step is all-important: you need to convince yourself you're going to set out to do it. **You have to make a commitment; you have to believe in yourself and set some kind of a goal**. It's something like taking a trip. When you decide to go somewhere you've never been before, you have to pull out a road map and take a look at the terrain between here and there. With the aid of that road map, you know exactly which highways you need to take to get where you want to go.

That's really how simple it is. You just have to start, and you do that by making a decision to start. **Everything has to come from some desire and then there has to be movement.** So many people have the desire alone, but no idea how to get that movement started. Well, the desire must push you into starting. <u>You have to make the decision that you're going to do it, that you have the desire, and then you actually have to take action</u>.

Here's a good way to kick start yourself: subscribe to at least three or four of the many opportunity magazines out there, like Money-Making, Entrepreneur, Inc., Small Business Opportunities, etc.; the list goes on and on. Go over each issue with a fine-toothed comb. **Write or call for free information on various moneymaking plans.** Some of those plans are excellent; some aren't very good at all. Nevertheless, send for these plans, so you can look at all the different opportunities other people are offering. At the same time, start reading some of the better books on business. I'm not talking about the ones by drones who were cogs in some giant corporation; I mean those written by guys who got their hands dirty and built their businesses from the ground up. If you decide to go the information or mail order route, start reading books on those subjects. **You have to learn before you can earn.**

Then, too, you should realize that confusion and frustration aren't altogether a bad thing. I know it's painful to be confused about what you want to do first -- and **when you follow my advice and start reading a lot of books, and start sending away for a lot of different opportunities, you might become even more confused for a while**. But you need to go with it. It'll eventually start coming together. If you can just keep that faith and keep those goals in front of you, things will become clearer as you move forward.

Most people are so confused about what they need to do to get started that they never get past Step One. They'll start doing some preparation, start sending away for all kinds of opportunities, and then get so confused that they get all frustrated and quit. **What I like to teach people is that success is a lot like driving at night**. It may be the darkest night of the year, but even if you have to drive 200 miles down the road, all you need to do is jump in your car and go. Proceed cautiously, of course; don't overdrive your headlights. You'll be able to see a little bit in front of you all the time; but as long as you know where your destination is and follow the route on your map, you'll get there, assuming you drive safely and follow some basic rules of the road. **You may start out in darkness, but a good plan will give you a way to get from here to there.**

There's no perfect time to start a business, but a lot of people are waiting for that perfect time anyhow. **They have the delusion that someday, things are going to be just right and they're going to get into business for themselves**. But I like to teach people that there is no perfect time. Here's an example. We did a seminar in Kansas City once, and we had a gentleman there who was 89 years old. It was a 2 ½ day seminar, and I kept an eye on him -- because it was so inspirational to me that somebody that old would invest in this seminar, which cost $4,950.

This gentleman had invested a sizable chunk of money into learning what we were teaching and he was taking far more notes than most of the other attendees were. He was sitting right up front. What that said to me was that he wasn't letting his age stop him from learning everything he could, which is exactly how you should view this. **Getting started is half the battle.** There's never a perfect time; you're never too young and you're never too old.

Age stops a lot of people. Some think that they're too young when, in fact, I know entrepreneurs who started their careers when they were teens. Most people in their 80s would say they're too old for something like this, but that's not true either. **There's never a perfect time or age to start; and there's never a horrible time**. It's kind of like that famous opening line in A Tale of Two Cities: "It was the best of times; it was the worst of times." Every era, every decade, combines a little of the worst and a little of the best.

You just have to make a commitment and be willing to do whatever it takes. I like what entrepreneur Joe Cossman says. Joe started with virtually no money and went on to earn millions. His favorite quote is, "Everything is hard until it become easy." I often use that quote myself. The point is, there's nothing so hard that it can't become easy once you get the hang of it. For example: Russ von Hoelscher is one of the highest-paid copywriters in the country right now. He gets paid thousands of dollars for putting together just one direct mail package. I happen to know that, nowadays, it's something that comes relatively easy to him. But it wasn't always like that. **He even has a joke he tells people sometimes: that every direct mail package he produces takes him 10 hours and 32 years to actually produce.** It depends on how you look at it. Someone will say, "Gee, I'm paying you $5,000 and you're doing this in a day or two, and probably only worked on it 10 or 12 hours. What's the deal here?" Sure, you paid him $4,000 or $5,000 for 10 or 12 hours work -- but there's also 32 years in there when he was learning to do it, and you didn't pay him anything! **You're paying Russ not just for the hours of work he put into it, but for all that experience as well.**

Remember: everything that's easy to him he had to struggle with at one time. A premium direct mail package might have taken him three or four weeks to do at one time, not a day or two -- and he made half as much as he does now, or less. It's an evolutionary process. It'll be the same with you. **You'll start to think about what business to start in, what you should sell, and we're going to point you in the right direction -- _but you're going to be amazed at how easy it's going to become_, once you sift through all this stuff and get past the difficult phase.** The difficult phase is always the first several months, when you're learning, and you go two steps forward and two steps back. Pretty soon you'll be taking two steps forward and one step back; then, eventually, hopefully, you'll get ten steps forward for every step back.

Also, your understanding of the business will develop and mature as you go along. A lot of things in life are that way. Let's say, for instance, that you decide you're going to learn how to master the game of chess. Chess is a game with a great many potential moves on the board, despite the fact that there are relatively few pieces in play. I learned the game because somebody sat down, spent 30 minutes showing me the basic moves, and then played a game with me where they helped me make all of the moves. Within an hour I was actually playing chess myself. Now, I wasn't any good at it -- but chess is one of those games that takes a lifetime to master. **And the truth is: to be good at something you have to practice constantly, so you get better as time goes on.** There are people who spend their entire lives learning to master the game of chess. I'm talking about spending years just thinking about all the different moves and mastering the various kinds of strategies. Some of these chess masters have 87 different ways that they can just do the opening moves of the game.

Making money is a lot like that, at least in the way successful entrepreneurs think about it. Consider this analogy deeply. You might be confused now, but the more you learn and study, and the more you work through that confusion, the more you're going to learn new key strategies everywhere you go. **Eventually, if you're just willing to stay in the game, you're going to have the exact winning combination you need.** You'll be just like one of those chess masters who can sit down and beat you in four moves. And making money really is kind of like a game -- a fun, exhilarating, exciting game where you keep score by how much money you make.

Of course, you'll eventually learn that money won't make you happy, which is a great revelation. At first it's a bitter pill to swallow; if you're like me, all of your life you thought, "Gosh, if I just had more money, if I could just become a millionaire, I'd just be so happy." Then, when you reach that plateau, when you have a nice house and a new

Cadillac (or whatever rich means to you), you look at yourself in the mirror and say, "Wow, is that all there is?" That's when the game either gets depressing or more exciting. **You've realized that money is great, but it's not going to make you happy**. It's just going to give you more toys, more opportunities, and more options in your life. Money will NOT make you happy, but you have to have a lot of it before you realize that. Once you do, you can look at making money more as a game -- the most enjoyable game on the planet -- and focus on all the good you can do with it.

At M.O.R.E. Inc. we're in the direct response marketing business. When you're in this business, you make most of your money from the promotions you create or the products and services that you sell. It's the things that you do to earn the money that becomes part of the game. **It's learning how to master those things that makes you a success and it all starts with knowledge: <u>the knowledge of how to run your business in the best possible way</u>**. The Bible says, "Seek ye first the Kingdom of Heaven and all else shall be added..." In business, I think that we can say, "Seek ye first the knowledge of how to run a successful business, and all of the secrets and success will be revealed."

One of the things that we've realized is that most (if not all) of the people we've met who are making huge amounts of money tend to look at it as a fun process. A lot of the business people we meet are having the times of their lives. They're actively involved in their business. **They're excited about the products and services that their company sells so it's not work to them.** It's almost the opposite of work. <u>They love their customers and they love every aspect of what they're doing</u>. Sure, they have their tough days, but that's part of playing the game, too. When you play any kind of game or sport, you realize that there are times when you have to suffer some losses. It's not a perfect life; it's more of a lifestyle than a job.

If you're happy working nine-to-five five days a week, just getting by, but having all your evenings and all your weekends to yourself, then don't get into business. When we talk about freedom in business, we mean that you can take off many days that someone who works for someone else can't -- but some Saturdays you'll be working while they're out playing. **You have to enjoy what you're doing**. Just think of the opportunities that are available to you that will not be available when you're working for someone else.

When you enjoy what you're doing, it's not really work! That's such a valuable thing to consider. If you can get to this point, your work is almost like a hobby. **When people ask what my wife Eileen and I do with all our time, we tell them that our work for M.O.R.E., Inc. is more like a lifestyle that we live, or a hobby that we do**. People do hobbies for fun. They spend a lot of time and money on their hobbies and they invest a lot of themselves in their hobbies. They're passionately enthused about what it is that they do, whether it's photography or woodworking or even collecting baseball cards. Well, that's the way our business is to us. **And let me interject this key point here: the hobbies you love can also make you rich.** Think in terms of what you really love as a hobby, if you have one. Many people, from writers to collectors to entrepreneurs, have turned their hobbies into millions of dollars of income.

Chapter Two

Get Started

Step #1 of my four-step Fast Track to Riches is **"Prepare Yourself."** Get started, take that first step, and set the goal that you're going to go out and make a lot of money. Get your attitude right. Understand that there's some investment here of yourself and definitely a change of lifestyle involved.

Now it's time for Step #2: **"Pick your market and develop some kind of an initial front-end offer."** Just jump in and get started. That's the foundation of all businesses: just get started. Prepare yourself, then actually make the commitment; follow through and do it. That's where it helps if you're involved with something that you really love, like a hobby. You're able to put your passion into what you do.

If you don't have a vigorous hobby, or don't think your hobbies can be made profitable, then you might want to sign up for a turn-key distributorship. There are dozens of them out there. You decide which field you prefer -- whether that's mail order, import/export, flea markets, swap meets, selling close-out stuff, or whatever else you'd like to do. Find out if someone's offering books or tapes on the subject, or offering a distributorship where you can sell their books or tapes, or their merchandise if you decide to go with that end of it. It's easy to get started and doesn't necessarily cost you much to get involved. In fact, it's a good way to get your feet wet in business without much risk -- and it's a great way to learn on the job.

Before you get into business on your own, you have to ask yourself some very basic questions. First, ask yourself, **"Do I really want to do this? Does this excite me? Can I get out of bed in the morning and say 'Hello world! I'm ready for you!'?"** That's a very important first step. Then you have to start asking practical, pragmatic questions like, <u>"Which people are likely to purchase my products or services? What are their mindsets, wants and desires, hopes and fears? How can I address them, offer them something they need, and convince them with my sales materials that they really need it?"</u> Then, of course, you need to think of advertising and marketing. **"How can I attract business from these people? Where do I find them? How do I get them to buy from me?"**

All these things have been answered by every successful business out there. As long as you know that, you'll start to see how other businesses are using those concepts. **You can take ideas that other companies or other individuals are using and then find all the ways you can develop those ideas for yourself**. It's a valuable short-cut technique in your business education. That's another reason why you want to be on all those mailing lists and calling up or writing those companies of interest to you. <u>You want to see just what they're doing, what they're offering, and how they're offering it.</u> You want to model your business after the most successful ones in the same field, or a similar one.

All of us are in business for the same reason: <u>generating a profit.</u> That's what we have to do. We all have customers we're trying to serve with some product or service and we want to do it in a unique enough way that they'll continue to do more business with us. That's the common denominator of all business. Although that might sound simplistic, and it may sound like common sense, I promise you that there are a lot of books out there on how to make money in your own business that never put it that clearly. A lot of those books are written by college professors or managers of Fortune 500 companies. They're overcomplicated and they're not talking about small business at all. No, you need to get books by entrepreneurs who've traveled the same road. They not only "talk the talk," but they "walk the walk." There's a big different between them and someone who's running General Motors or IBM. Many of those people are talking about things that we, as entrepreneurs, probably don't need to know right now. **We have to learn how to get down and dirty and start from scratch and how to keep it simple -- almost in a cookbook fashion**. Now, eventually, you'll take a detour on these paths. You'll find some techniques that work for you that aren't in the books, but you want instructions that are easy to follow when you're first starting.

Here are a couple of easy-to-follow instructions. First of all, the process of marketing is very simple. It involves two steps, the first of which is all the things you do to attract new customers to you. Second, it's all of the things you do to keep those customers coming back and doing more business with you. That's all that marketing is, especially at first. **You have to get the right message to the right people through the right media**. If I want to sell something to photographers -- for example, if I want to show photographers how they can turn a hobby into a moneymaking business -- I'm going to give them 101 ways to make money with their camera, even if they're amateurs now. I'm going to show them how to make some really good money. **That's the message, but I have to know where those photographers -- my "right people" -- are**. In this case, we know they're going to be reading the photography magazines; we know we can mail to lists of amateur photographers. That's going to make it pretty simple to get my message before the right audience, through the right media.

For some products, services, and information, however, it's not as easy to know exactly where the right people are and how to best reach them. Let's say you're selling wrist watches imported from Hong Kong. You got a great deal on them and they have all kinds of gizmos and alarms. So far, so good. **Now, where are the right people and the right media for those watches?** You might say to yourself, "Well, almost everybody wears a wristwatch, so I guess that every medium's the right medium." Wrong! Danger signals! The bells should be going off at that point. It's true that almost everybody drives a car, almost everybody has a wristwatch, almost everybody eats three times a day -- <u>but you usually can't take that broad knowledge and turn it into money</u>. If you have a really unique novelty-type watch, you have to think in terms of high-tech publications. You should also be thinking in terms of upscale publications, although a $50 watch is actually pretty cheap. You should be thinking of science and mechanical publications. **In order to do well, you'll need to do some serious thinking about where to find the people who want what you're offering.**

One of the reasons we teach people to go with something they already know or love is because a lot of those questions are already answered for them. For example, if you're a woodworker, then you already know the publications other woodworkers might be attracted to. **It's better to stick with things you know and keep this in mind: there are a million different things you can do to make money.** <u>The trick is to find the right things</u>. If you stick closer with the things you're interested in now, know about now, or have some passion for, then you stand a better chance of hitting major success. The more you know the market and the more you know the people in the market and can really get inside their heads and their hearts, the more effectively you can sell to them.

So pick your market and develop some type of initial way to attract customers. You can learn how to do that better simply by watching how other people do it. **Answer the ads, stop looking at other businesses as a consumer looks at businesses, get on the other side of the cash register, and see how other companies are attracting their customers**. Get your ideas there. That's the best way that you can learn.

Take advantage of what Russ von Hoelscher calls the "funnel concept." **In simple terms: you cast your nets out there in the best publications, or use direct mail or card decks or some other method to market your product or service.** To start off, offer something very inexpensive or free, such as a free report that's really a combination report and glorified sales letter. You're throwing your net out to sea and you're dragging in first dozens, then hundreds, and hopefully, eventually, thousands of prospects. You'll find that only a certain number are keepers. If you were a fisherman, you'd decide what to keep and what to throw back. It's similar for us: a certain small percentage of all potential customers will actually become our customers. We start by drawing our pool of potential customers into a huge funnel, and then the pool gets smaller and smaller as we go along. **As we decrease that pool, we start doing more business with a certain percentage of our customers**. Then we use our back-end products to get the second and third sale. This is where the old 80/20 rule comes into effect. Twenty percent of your customers will probably give you 80% of your business. That's why you bring in as many as you can; you have to constantly add new people and new leads in order to find the good ones. It's a continual process of filling the funnel at the top, where the funnel represents the big universe of customers that you're attracting. Then it's about coming more into focus with those who choose to do business with you. You do everything you can to make them want to buy from you again and again.

Chapter Three

Advertising

As a business owner, you constantly have to do things to attract new customers. That's the third step in the Fast Track to Riches system. **Once you've developed a way to attract customers and sell them something, you have to make a commitment and run the actual advertising or promotion that brings people to you.** It doesn't even have to be very expensive; in fact, we teach people <u>NOT to start out with expensive advertising</u>. Start with classified ads, which are among the cheapest ads you'll ever use. Use voicemail to collect contact e-mail addresses and phone numbers from the people who raise their hands and ask for more information. **Encourage people to call rather than write -- although if you have the space and it doesn't cost too much, it's a good idea to put both the snail-mail address and phone number in the advertisement.** Then, when they call or write, you have a legitimate lead. There are a lot of companies and individuals out there who are making tremendous amounts of money by running these small ads.

We also teach people the concept of small streams, an analogy that comes from a couple of books on Warren Buffet, one of the richest people in the world. Buffet is a billionaire who lives in Omaha, Nebraska; he's been in the investment business now since the early 1950s, and he's made billions of dollars. When you study his strategy, you'll find that it's basically very simple. He owns various stocks in all these different companies. He picks them very carefully, and buys them properly. He's in it for the long haul. Instead of looking for the right business opportunity, he searches for the best companies that show several years of accelerated earnings and increases in the value of the shares. **As long as he earns a steady stream of income from all these little investments, when those streams all come together he creates a giant river that has produced billions of dollars in wealth for him**. He's also made many other people multi-millionaires.

That same concept can apply to small ads, too. Let's say you're running 100 small ads. Each of those 100 ads is bringing in a small income stream. Taken together, they can create a giant flood of income. **It's all about quality and quantity.** Now, our business is a little bit different from Buffett's; we're looking for markets, while Buffet and other great stock pickers are looking for investments. In our case, it's more important to know markets than it is to know anything else in business. **First you find the market, determine that enough people are in it, and know that it's a defined market that you can reach**. Once you know a market's out there and there's a way and a means to reach it, you can start running your ads, and start tweaking them, and chipping away at that marketplace.

A market is just a group of people who have something in common, and there's almost always some way to reach them. If you wanted to develop a business that served woodworkers, you would find that there are about a dozen publications that serve them. There are a few big ones and a bunch of smaller ones; that goes for almost any narrow niche market. So you know that there's a group of people who have something in common, based on the specific interest they share. <u>There are certain publications that they read and there are certain mailing lists that apply to them.</u> There are all kinds of ways to reach specific types of individuals. Remember, we're talking about niche markets.

The scariest thing in the world to a marketing person is a HUGE market. Someone might come to me (as they have over the years, many times) and say, "I have a book on how to save money when you buy a used car." Well, okay, people want to save money on used cars; I know that that's true. I also know that every year, millions of people buy used cars. But selling a book like that is more challenging than going to woodworkers, photographers, hunters, fishermen, bowlers, or any one of 101 other niche markets. **When the market's broad and almost everybody could be a prospect, that's when you really have to put on your thinking cap.**

Sometimes you can target your market by advertising in certain sections of more general publications, too. **Newspapers are an excellent example; they represent a very broad medium, <u>but fortunately their advertising pages are divided into specific sections</u>**. If you wanted to sell a used car or even offer information on how to buy one, you wouldn't advertise in the general news section; you'd want to be in the classified section under "cars for sale." We've had distributors who did very well selling a book on home employment and they advertised in the "Help Wanted" section of the newspapers. The only people reading that section were people who were legitimately looking for a way to make extra money; otherwise, they wouldn't have been looking there. By placing the advertisement in the "Help Wanted" section, our distributors were able to reach the group of people who were most likely to buy that publication. <u>Millions of dollars worth of books were sold, using that very simple technique.</u>

Part of Step #3 is testing. There are lots of entrepreneur magazines out there -- Spare Time, Money Making Opportunities, Opportunity Magazine, etc. -- but they may not all be appropriate for what you have to offer. Certain publications might be better for certain types of moneymaking offers. If it's a get-rich book, it might work better dollar-for-dollar if you advertise in Money Making Opportunities. Conversely, if it's a more substantial plan or home study course that deals with a more elaborate type of business opportunity, then perhaps Entrepreneur Magazine or some of the success magazines might be better. You have to decide what will work best for you.

Because you don't necessarily know everything about your market, you should run your classified ad once in order to find out which approach works best. **Keep the word-length and the cost down because you might have to change that ad**. You might have to place it in more publications. We might have to take some out of the equation. Key your ad to make sure that it's working. Test all kinds of things: not just the publication, but the ad itself. **<u>Remember, the classified ad is basically a headline with a way to respond.</u>** One ad that Russ ran for a long time was "Free Report -- How to Get Rich on the Information Superhighway," and then the phone number. That makes the most exceptional and best-working kind of classified ad. Give them a dynamite headline and a phone number, unless you have the luxury of also providing an address. Just to show you how simple it can be, that one little ad has generated hundreds of thousands of dollars in sales.

In some cases, it costs very little to place an ad like this, though in national publications like USA Today or Entrepreneur you can spend hundreds of dollars per issue. But it may cost less than $50 in a smaller targeted publication. Maybe for that price, you get one person who buys your product for $197. It doesn't take rocket science to realize that this can be extremely lucrative.

Here's another important point that needs to be

brought up: in testing, it's vital to know that the customer's always the boss. It's not our ideas that count; we have great ideas all the time. We put these ideas for products and services that we think our customers would really want out there, based on our experience and knowledge of who our customers are, how we can best serve them, and give them more of what they really, really want. **Ultimately, the customer's the one who decides -- and sometimes they surprise us**. Sometimes we think we have the hottest thing ever, and the customer says, "So what?" Sometimes we don't think something's going to be that great and the customers just fall over themselves to get it.

Keep this in mind: the customer is in charge, and they tell you exactly what they want. **That's a key concept you should never, ever forget.** You don't make any money until something's sold. All selling is serving. You have to give people what they really want and help them get it in as many ways as you can. Eventually, you'll want to develop all kinds of related products and services for your customers. You're bringing those customers in through the large mouth of the funnel. You're attracting them with some initial offer. You're doing business with more of them -- then you resell to those customers again and again. **Selling is serving. Write that sentence down, carry it with you, and memorize it.** It's not just about trying to get that money in their wallet or their bank account. You're trying to get them to spend their money for something that's more valuable to them than the money that they have. You're trying to serve them. You're trying to give them something of real value; you're trying to help them get what they want most, in the form of your product or service. Again, the customer is the ultimate judge and jury and, as it turns out, some of our favorite ideas are the ones that are the most poorly received out there. Zig Ziglar used to say, "You can get anything you want out of life

as long as you FIRST help other people get what they want."
Now he modifies it to, "You can HAVE anything in life by
helping enough other people HAVE what they want."

Chapter Four

Get Your Back-End Together!

The fourth step in our Fast Track to Riches system is to getting your back-end together. Now, that's not a euphemism for getting your rear in gear, but it's something similar! Once you've prepared yourself with a game plan, developed a front-end product, and started running those targeted advertisements, you'll start building your customer list -- and those customers will be eager for you to keep building that relationship with them, and to offer them more products to make their lives better. This is where Step #4, building up your back-end, comes in -- and it's where all of the profits are to be made.

Here's why this fourth step is so crucial to the overall riches that can be made. **First of all, customer acquisition costs so much money that you'll often do no better than break even**. Many times you'll lose money, especially if you're offering something free. There's no way to get around that, so the profits have to come on the back-end. **The back-end simply involves selling that customer a bigger and better version of what you originally gave them, or selling them an extension of what they originally got.** The back-end is where you're able to put together something of value and get paid a good price for it, make a good profit, and yet still give the customer what they need. When we talk about back-ends, we also talk about back-ends to our back-ends. <u>We want a relationship with that customer that lasts</u>, one where we can go back to them on a regular basis with new materials, new services, new products, and continue to sell them. The profit with any customer is in their repeat buying from us. The back-end is the first major sale we make, but hopefully we can make many more.

When Russ von Hoelscher starting working with us back in the early 1990s, he was responsible for helping us earn millions of dollars; he really got us off the ground, though when he first started working with us, we were bringing in more money than we ever dreamed of making. **Yet within a nine month period, he had us up to almost $100,000 in sales every single week.** A lot of our customers and clients say, "How did Russ do that for you? What exactly did he do?" Well, although he did help us develop our front-end by helping us get into direct mail, which was a very important part of our overall success, **I'd have to say that his most important lesson was realizing the value of the back-end and showing us how to do it.**

The back-end is critical to financial success in business. The last effective entrepreneur who did without it in our business and got away with it was Joe Carbo. He sold so many copies of his book Lazy Man's Riches through newspaper and magazine ads that he didn't even need a back-end. He did eventually develop some back-ends, but they weren't that great. He didn't pursue them with the vigor that we do today. **He was able to sell millions of dollars worth of his book in the '70s, <u>but those days are gone</u>.**

Probably 99.99% of us make our money on the back-end today. Even in the 1960s and '70s only a small percentage of people made front-end profits alone; even then you needed a back-end. **Today you need it more than ever.** Most people have a service or product when we start working with them and they can't quite understand why they're not making money, especially if their service or product is moving quite well. The truth is most people don't realize that customer acquisition costs so much money. If you're selling a book for $20, once you go through all the costs to get that $20 order, you'll often find that you're spending $19 or $20 or maybe $21 or $22 to make every sale. You have the cost of the product, the cost of the mailing, and the cost of the advertising to deal with.

You must develop related products for the back-end in order to make any real money. This can transform a company that's making marginal profits into a million-dollar success. When someone buys something from you for $10, $20, or $30, or if you give them a free booklet or a free report and they really like it, they're motivated and excited and think your company is great. **That's the time you want to introduce them to a bigger and better offer on the back-end -- one that will enrich their lives tremendously, but also make you a big profit.**

So study what caused your customers to initially buy from you; try to get a real feel for what it was that drew them in the first time. **Then simply look for or develop products and services that give the customer more of what they initially bought the first time -- a bigger, better package that gives them more value and enriches their life even more.** At the same time it makes you, the dealer, money. When Russ started working with us, we were selling something called the Dialing for Dollars system. It was doing very well on the front-end and we'd developed something of a back-end. But when Russ got together with us, we enriched the back-end by bringing all kinds of new products and new books into the system -- eight of them at a time, once -- to make available to the people who bought the original Dialing for Dollars. We told them how they could make money with an answering machine or a voice mailbox, but then we were able to offer, eventually, dozens of printed products and information that they could sell on their own.

Many people don't want to develop their own products or services. That's why we offered them a wide array of products and services they could market and we always gave them good prices. All false modesty aside, our company's famous for that now. **We give the dealer much more than most companies would ever think of offering.** With Dialing for Dollars, we had the original sale, which was around $29.95, but many of our dealers would then spend four and five times more to get the complete package of dealership books and then many would go on to sell thousands and thousands of those books. The back-end just got bigger and better.

That strategy's really been responsible for our entire fortune. **Although at the time we were bringing in as many as 2,000 new customers every week, we were doing so at a loss -- we were losing money every single time.** We were mailing as many as a hundred thousand pieces a week (400,000 pieces of sales material every single month) and that was costing us an average of fifty cents apiece. So we were making an investment of $200,000 a month. **But even with all the new customers we were bringing in, we weren't able to recoup that entire investment!** In fact, we were fortunate if we could make maybe two-thirds of it back, and we were happy with that. We had to pay that investment month after month to attract and develop new customers. But through all these profitable avenues that Russ helped us develop, and all the back-end products and services that were related, we learned how to make a profit. He helped us develop a systematic approach to doing more business with the people we initially attracted.

Here's an example from Russ himself. Years ago, he was selling a video, first for $10 and later for $5. By the time he sent out that video, the total cost came to over $12. To the uninformed, that might look like sheer stupidity, but the truth was that about 7% of everyone who got that video later bought a $395 program, so Russ came out ahead. **That's why entrepreneurs are often willing to break even or even take a loss on the front-end, just to get a customer's name and address and get him to raise his hand**. We know he likes what we have or is interested in the topics that we're covering. It's up to us to give him something of value, so we have to give him a good sales message and get that back-end sale.

A lot of people hear that what you should do is look for ads that appear again and again. You should duplicate the products sold in those ads or come out with something very similar. **The danger is that many times -- almost all the time, actually -- the companies that run those ads month after month are really making their profits on the back-end**. So you need to study those companies as their customers, so you can learn how they're making their real profits. Those ads are just for attracting new customers -- and often they're coming in at a loss. You have to look at the total model, instead of assuming that these companies are successful just because of the ads that they run. I think you'd be amazed at how many companies are breaking even, at best, on the front end. If you were to just model yourself after what they're doing on the front-end and not develop a good back-end, you'd be making a terrible mistake. And of course, your back-end needs a back-end; I repeat that because it's so important.

You may see someone selling a book, for example, for $19.95. Let's say you've been seeing their ads for six months or a year, and you say to yourself, **"Heck, I think I can write a book like that, or get a ghostwriter to write it. I think the book will cost me $2 to publish and print. I'll sell it for $19.95. The profits are going to be great!"** Well, most of the time you're mistaken, my friend. The book might only cost $2 or $2.50 to print, and you might be able to ship it for another $2 or so, but the cost of advertising is so high today that if you try to sell a book for $19.95, thinking that your total cost is $4 or $5 and the rest is all profit, you're in for a rude awakening. You may be lucky to break even. **You might even have to spend $25 for every $19.95 book you sell.** The back-end, the big back-end, is where the money is.

Here's an ideal example, concerning a fellow from Illinois (for confidentiality reasons, I can't reveal his name here). Every month, he puts $20,000 a month in pure profits into his pocket. He starts by selling a $19.95 book in all the moneymaking magazines. He's been selling it for years now, using full-page ads. **That book gives the readers some good, solid information, and often leads to the sale of a more expensive home-study course.** I believe he has two different versions; one sells for under $500, the other for under $700.

Just by running that full-page ad in a few moneymaking magazines and selling his $19.95 book, when all is said and done, he's putting an average of $20,000 in profit in his pocket -- super-fast. **He usually gets that bigger sale within 10-15 days of the time that his book goes out to the customer.** That $20,000 a month, every single month, is pure profit from the sale of the bigger product. His $19.95 breaks even on the cost of the ad these days, though at one point he was able to make a profit on the book because it was so popular. **But with those $500 and $700 sales on the back-end, he's still making money hand over fist.** There are a lot of doctors and lawyers who'd be envious of that kind of income. They dream of someday being able to make that kind of income.

This gentleman has realized one of the basic realities of making money in our business: he sucks a lot of people into that big funnel with his front-end offer, then the funnel gets a little bit smaller, but a certain percentage of the people in the funnel come out the other side making those $500, $600, and $700 purchases. He closes as high as 10% of those sales, which is pretty amazing. **And now he's developing back-ends to his back-end.** He's doing seminars for his customers. He has special services and other products he's developing. His is a perfect story to illustrate the Fast Track to Riches.

What's more, his business plan is so simple that even a child could understand it. Let me repeat it here for emphasis. He runs a full-page ad in the moneymaking magazines. That ad sells a book. That book, which lays out a specific formula that he's developed in marketing and making money, sells the bigger package. **With a simple three-step system, he's putting the kind money in his pocket that, usually, only doctors and lawyers make.**

Here's another example: a dentist named Dr. Savaran. We helped him get out of dentistry, but he developed something that was related: a mini ID card, which simply involves putting a patient's history on a piece of Mylar and attaching it to a little 2 x 4 inch plastic card. Medical personnel can run it through a microfiche machine, and see what a person is allergic to or whatever. So he stuck with something related to the medical field, but it created a whole different profession for him. **He was able to come up with something that was unique and very successful, and went out and sold that product to many pharmacies and drug stores.**

Then he came up with another idea. **He didn't just want to be a person taking his little medical IDs around by foot, trying to get people to resell them for him -- so he got in the mail order business.** He started selling them first directly to the consumer, and then developed a complete dealership where other people did the same. His dealership became his back-end, and a tremendously profitable one.

Chapter Five

You Really Can Do It!

I've always found inspirational stories to be a great teaching tool. I'm not talking about Horatio Alger fables of how the nice boy makes good because his heart is pure and his spirit steadfast; I'm talking about real-live tales of people who started with nothing and built a fortune. For example, take several carpet cleaners that I happen to know. One is me. **Before I got involved in mail order in such a big, wonderful way, I owned a carpet cleaning business**. While I made some fairly good money, I found it to be very hard and not that profitable.

I know another carpet cleaner, Frank Pechazelli from Santa Anna, California, who hated carpet cleaning. He came to Russ several years ago and said, "I'm getting out of this darn business. My back hurts. The business gives me a headache. I'm through with it, Russ. Help me get in the mail order business." **He was surprised when Russ told him that it was possible to make money teaching others to do what you don't personally want to do anymore.** To make a long story short, Russ got Frank Pechazelli involved in the mail order publishing business selling a manual on *"How to Be a Carpet Cleaner."* He didn't want to do it himself anymore -- but that didn't mean he can't teach others to do it. He went so far as offering other manuals and newsletters on the back-end and also went all the way to procuring cleaning supplies and hospital supplies and making them available at a discount to dealers. It's a tremendous back-end profit-maker for him.

Then there's Joe Polish, who was in the carpet cleaning business too. He doesn't hate the business because it's been good to him. He's also taught other people how to get in the carpet cleaning business on the back-end. **The big back-end to the back-end is that he's becoming the carpet cleaners' guru**. He holds seminars and has books, tapes, and newsletters he's sending out all over the country, not only teaching people how to get into the carpet cleaning business but also showing them how to make maximum profits. **He shares with them all the tricks, tips, techniques, and strategies he knows, so that their business can double and triple.**

Pechazelli hated the business, but then learned how to make money with it, but Joe Polish has become the guru of carpet cleaners. **Now, all Joe's doing is taking good, solid marketing ideas that are readily available and adapting them to the carpet cleaning service business**. All the carpet cleaners who've never been exposed to those great marketing ideas think Joe is a genius. Having met Joe, I can say this: he does have a great amount of intelligence -- you have to have that -- but he's no genius. He just has a lot of courage; that's his whole formula. **He's not afraid to get out there and try something, and he speaks the language of the other carpet cleaners.** Joe has told me that, in his best months, he's putting $40,000 a month in his pocket after all his expenses. This is one guy who only has one employee. That's it. That's incredible money. What's really incredible is that the same marketing tips and strategies he's giving to carpet cleaners can be applied by people in all kinds of service industries. They can be used for any profession there is.

While we're on the subject of cleaning carpets, let me discuss our carpet cleaning adventure for a bit. Our story illustrates the simple fact that you don't need very much money to get started. That's the one thing that hangs a lot of people up; they think you need a lot of money to get started. When I started the carpet cleaning business, before I met Eileen (and if it wasn't for the carpet cleaning business, I might never have met her), I was cleaning carpets for another company. I saw how easy and simple it was. I was booking all my own jobs and my boss was supplying me with the equipment. I learned how to get in there and sell carpet cleaning jobs. I was responsible for all of the business I generated -- **but while I did all of the work, my boss got 40% of every dollar that I made and all I was doing was using his equipment and his truck**. Basically, I got tired of that. I dreamed of being in a business of my own.

I went out with basically no money at all, found a van that was for sale (the guy wanted $600 for the most beat-up van, but it was something), and I offered him $1,000 for it if he'd let me make payments. I paid $100 every week. He readily agreed. We worked out a contract where if I missed one of my payments, he'd take the van back. He knew where I lived.

Then I went to a janitorial supply company and got them to give me some equipment; again, it was on a payment plan where there was no cash out-of-pocket. Then I went to a printer and did the same thing. . The printer printed some flyers for me on credit. **I had no money to speak of, but with no money at all up front, I was in the carpet cleaning business, after doing it for a just few months for another company!** It wasn't the greatest business on Earth, but at least it got me started. That's what you really need to do. You need to get started, no matter where you're at. Then you develop the confidence that's necessary to go on to bigger and better things.

Something else I find exciting is the whole

concept of turning adversity into success. Here's a story I heard from Russ about someone he knows well. This guy was a preacher, he was preaching the gospel at some small non-denominational church in a little town in Alabama, and he had a wife and a couple of sweet little daughters. Then all of a sudden, for whatever reason, his wife said, "I don't like this life." He was hardly making any money; they were barely getting by. They truly were as poor as church mice and she just took off.

So here he was stuck with the kids and not making any money as the preacher of this little, tiny church. He got himself in trouble; he got his credit all screwed up and it was a mess. But then he dug his way out. **He learned so much about credit and about people who got in debt that he started selling books on credit repair.** He became a real expert on that and also on other ways to get out of debt. He's gone on to make a ton of money with that, mostly by putting good back-ends together. His customers might initially buy a credit repair book for $25, but on the back-end he offers some advanced home-study courses that can help you really clean up your credit quickly. Now he's wealthy and successful, just a few years after he lost his wife, got in terrible trouble with his credit, and had bill collectors pounding on the door and calling on the phone. It's so exciting how he took that adversity and turned it into profit. **He started, very simply, by running some classified ads in some local newspapers**. He had a two-page report that he either sold by itself or that helped him sell an initial product to the customer.

I know another guy named Ted Thomas who often tells his story at conventions and seminars. Ted owned a small aircraft dealership in San Francisco and was a millionaire back then. As things got bad in the late '70s and the early '80s, he lost everything. He went from being a millionaire to being deep in debt. He had a lot of foreclosures on properties that he owned. So what did he do? He learned everything he could about foreclosures, the same thing he faced, and started helping other people get out of foreclosures -- or in many cases, buying their homes or condos and paying them some money, whereas they would get no money if they waited for the sheriff to throw them out. **Later, with the help of Russ and some other marketing people, he became the #1 foreclosure expert in the country, selling a book on the front-end and then having several great home-study courses and seminars on the back-end.**

So as you can see, even if you're digging your way out of a hole, it doesn't have to be all that complicated. **It can be as simple as putting together an initial product and then running some small classified ads**. Eileen and I had a distributor in Provo, Utah, who did just that very simple thing. He took a couple of the publications we produced for all our distributors and started running some ads, testing as many different ads as he possibly could. He worked this very hard and, in his best year, he did over $5 million in sales. On the back-end, he hardly did anything. **This man actually found a way -- although I wouldn't advise this -- to make money on the front-end by experimenting with various scripts, sales letters, and sales material**. By using newspapers, which offer a very inexpensive form of advertising, he was bringing in millions of dollars. A lot of that was pure profit, too. I know that at one point, he had $7 million sitting in the bank.

It can be done, folks. **The most important thing this guy did differently from all our other distributors is that he thought bigger.** With this big thinking he had, he tried all kinds of things until he found the right formula for making money. **You should do the same: think big, keep trying**

new things, and keep experimenting to find out what's possible. And remember those two gentlemen I told you about, the preacher and the airplane salesman? Both of them started out deep in the hole, and ended up making millions of dollars. I'm especially impressed with the preacher, who started with just $100 worth of classified advertising. In the beginning he used a lot of newspapers; he started out with just a few, but it had such a tremendous affect that he multiplied three papers to six to ten to 20 to 40 and eventually turned $100 into millions.

Russ also has a story about an old friend of his named Steve Lockman. We've known Steve for over a decade now, thanks to Russ. **For a long time things just weren't working out right for Steve; then, all of a sudden, something amazing happened.** About 20 years ago, Steve was working almost exclusively for Russ, writing some of his booklets and books. Basically, everything he had back then was coming from Russ. Now, Steve is a great person, but he'd gone through some hardships in his life. He's also had a few medical problems that he's had to overcome. **Life just wasn't going so good for him back then -- and things continued like that for a while because he wasn't really taking the initiative.**

Back when Steve and Russ were kids, Steve was a very good poet, and when he got a little older, he was quite the ladies' man. He'd write poetry for the girls and they would just love it. Later, he was able to go from writing short stories and poetry to being able to write full-size business books. **About fifteen years ago, he finally took the initiative and started running little classified ads in various newspapers and especially in writer-type publications.** He also runs ads in some of the business publications, like Success and Entrepreneur magazine. He's spending a few hundred dollars on these little classified ads, offering his ghostwriting and copywriting services.

He continues to surprise me. Someone in England saw his ad in Success a few years back and gave him this big job writing an investment course. I said, "What is that going to pay you?" and he said, "Oh, $6,000." Steve used to be happy to work for a couple of hundred dollars for a ghostwriting job. Now he's getting paid $5,000 and $6,000. He's making a lot of money now and it couldn't happen to a nicer guy. **He's taken a talent that he's always had and just by honing it -- not by going to school and taking big journalistic courses -- he's become a very talented ghostwriter with clients all over the world.** Steve wrote some of the initial publications our distributors sold. The work he was doing for us at that time went for several hundred dollars; now we'd be lucky if we could get him to do something for a couple thousand.

Steve told us a story once that really stuck in my mind. Again, everything didn't start changing for him until about 15 years ago. He told us he had some serious medical problems, he ended up in the hospital, and he thought he was going to die. During that period, he just rethought his whole life and began seeing some of the problems he was having with not getting himself motivated. I think a lot of people have the same kind of problem as he did initially. **But then he made a decision that nothing was going to stop him**. From that point on, he started doing things differently. Instead of waiting for Russ to bring jobs to him, he started running his own classified ads and landing his own work. Steve's business model is very simple. All he's doing is running some small classified ads. People who are interested in his services call him. He has no big expenditures at all. In fact, he probably makes about $1,000 for every $10 in advertising. Not many of us could match that. That's just fabulous, and it all came about because he finally got fed up with whatever it was that was holding him back. **He got sick and tired of being sick and tired**. He decided to take some initiative and go out and do it. He always had the talent and the ability.

The lesson to the reader is: **Don't wait for things to happen**. A lot of people are waiting. They're expecting someone else to bring them the goods. That's not going to happen, my friend. **You have to take the initiative**. Sometimes it can be just as simple as putting together a little program and running a few cheap classified ads. Like Nike tells us, Just do it. In Chapter 1 I mentioned an older gentleman who came to a mail order seminar I was giving. He said to me, "You know, I've been thinking about starting some type of business for about 50 years. Now I think that I'm really going to do it." I encouraged him to do it, but I really felt like saying to him, "Mister, you're not going to have another 80 years to think about it!" **The idea is to TAKE ACTION!** When you take action, even if you don't know all the answers (and you'll never know all the answers), things just start to happen, you're moving forward and that's a major key to success.

There's a man named Mark Nolan in Sacramento, California. For years, Mark did consulting work for various companies, until he found a couple of his clients who were doing extremely well with certain products and promotions. Mark said, "To heck with this. I'm not going to be a consultant anymore." At the time he was earning decent money; in a good year, he would earn $70,000 or $80,000 a year. **Simply by watching what a couple of his clients were doing and modeling his actions after them, he's now totally on his own**. His income has tripled and he's working fewer hours, has fewer headaches, he's able to spend more time with his family, and he's staying open to what other people are doing. That's the thing. A lot of people dream of having a business that does a million a year, but they've never asked themselves, "Okay, what will I have to do to get it?" Well, once you start asking yourself that question and break it all down, you'll see that it can really be quite simple.

Earlier we used the example of the man in Illinois who sells a $19.95 book and has two different products put together for the back end. The people who buy his book can choose one of his packages that sells for around $500, or another one that sells for around $700. **Just to show our listeners how easy it is to bring in a million dollars a year, all you have to do is sell seven $500 products a day, Monday through Saturday, six days a week**. Do that and you're going to bring in over $20,000 a week, which is over $1 million every single year. That's just seven products a day, 42 a week.

The question, then, is this: how many $19.95 products do you have to sell to sell those seven back-end products? If you're closing 10% like he is, then you have to sell 70 $19.95 books every single day, Monday through Saturday, to sell the seven $500 packages that will earn you the $20,000 a week in overall sales. **A great deal of that can be pure profit, as long as you're breaking even on your $19.95**. By using that example, I just wanted to show you exactly how simple and easy it really can be. How do you sell 70 $19.95 books then? That becomes the next question. How many ads do you have to run? What do you have to do to sell these 70 books every single day? You know, through testing, that if you sell 70 books a day, you're going to get an average of 7 sales at $500 apiece and you're going to put $20,000 a week into your bank account -- and be able to keep a good deal of it, if you can come close to breaking even on that $19.95 sale.

You can even lose money. Now, when you're first starting out and money's tight, we hate to talk about losing money. But eventually you build up some resources. Once you know that one out of every ten people buys a $500 product after buying the initial $19.95 book, then you can look at that $19.95 sale and say, "Yes, we'd like to make a profit, or at the very least break even, but because of that $500 and $700 sale on the back-end, we could even pay $25 to get that $19.95 sale and still make a lot of money."

I want to end this book with a simple idea. **Here it is: a lot of people dream about making money, but there seems to be this myth that those who are making huge amounts of money are somehow different than we are**. Well, all the rich people that Eileen and I have met since 1988, people who have been in the business for decades, people who are extremely successful -- they're all just ordinary people. Yes, they're very knowledgeable about what they do and they have a lot of experience and confidence. **But once you get to know them as people, you find out, "Hey, they're no different than I am!"**

That's one revelation Eileen and I want to pass along to you. All of the dozens of successful people we've met, including many who are millionaires in the same business that we're in, are people who are just like we are. **They're a very ordinary kind of people who just had a passion to get involved in business**. So they got involved, practiced the ideas that we've discussed here, and now they're millionaires. Russ von Hoelscher and most of our other colleagues and friends have found the same thing to be true. **Russ mentioned meeting a gentleman worth over $100 million and being surprised at how down-to-earth he was.** He could have anything that he wanted in the world, but he was talking about how a certain type of hotdog was his favorite, and on and on.

The truth is that when you strip away all the layers of preconceived ideas that you have about them, some of the richest people, some of the nicest people, and some of the smartest people in the world are just plain folks. It works the other way, too: some of the phoniest people you can meet, some of the people who seem to be successful and seem to be walking around in the clouds -- once you get to know them, you find they're just about one mortgage payment away from bankruptcy. They can't afford that Rolls Royce or that Mercedes Benz they're driving.

Still, some of the nicest and richest people are just plain folks and that's the way it should be. They're people who've done what I've tried to tell you about in this book. They've all practiced these four steps in some way. They got on the Fast Track to Riches and they made it happen! **You can do the very same thing if you're willing to work hard and follow these tips.** Go back, read this publication again, and take notes. Practice the ideas that I've shared with you here. I think you'll learn a lot in the process -- and I truly believe that something I've said will spark an idea in your mind that gives you the wherewithal to go forward on your own Fast Track to Riches.